SONNETS
FROM
THE PORTUGUESE

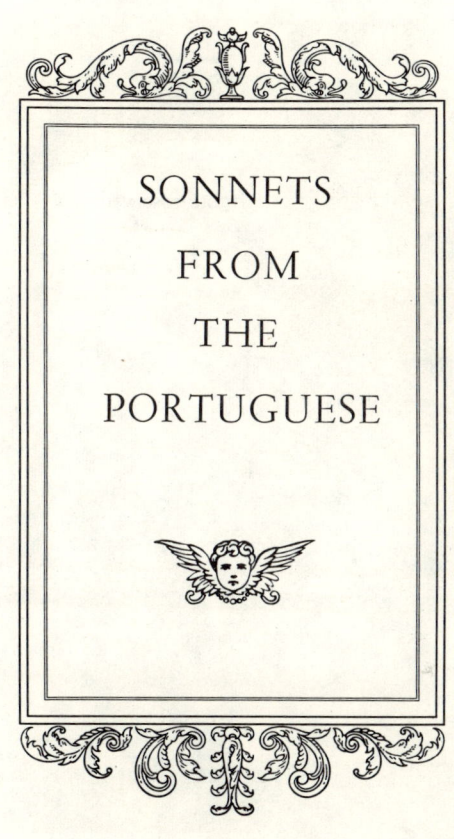

SONNETS FROM THE PORTUGUESE

By
ELIZABETH BARRETT BROWNING
Illustrations By FRED A. MAYER

AVENEL BOOKS
A DIVISION OF CROWN PUBLISHERS, INC.
NEW YORK

All rights reserved.

A NOTE

When Robert Browning met Elizabeth Barrett Moulton-Barrett for the first time, she had been for many years an invalid in her home at 50 Wimpole Street. The exact nature of her illness is uncertain. Mr. G. K. Chesterton says of her: 'She was an invalid, and an invalid of a somewhat unique kind, and living beyond all question under very unique circumstances'; and he speaks later of 'hysteria' and 'neurosis.' But whatever her illness may have been it was real enough to her, and dangerously so at times. 'The picture of helpless indolence' she calls herself; 'sublimely helpless and impotent'; 'I had done *living* I thought'; 'Was ever life so like death before? My face was so close against the tombstones, that there seemed no room even for the tears.' The thought comes often in the sonnets:

> Betwixt me and the dreadful outer brink
> Of obvious death, where I, who thought to sing . . .
>
> I yield the grave for thy sake, and exchange
> My near sweet view of Heaven, for earth with thee!

> Nor God's infliction, nor death's neighbourhood . . .

She speaks always of her life before the meeting with Browning as one of sadness:

> The sweet, sad years, the melancholy years,
> Those of my own life . . .

> Alas, I have grieved so I am hard to love.

>   For frequent tears have run
> The colours from my life . . .

Yet her childhood, passed on her father's country estate, was a happy one, until at the age of fifteen the illness which was to haunt her life began. At this time too while saddling her pony she injured herself in some way which was thought to have affected her spine, and this increased the delicacy of her health. She was a precocious child, who read Greek and wrote verses from very early days. A few years after the accident her mother died, and there remained to Elizabeth eight younger brothers, two sisters—and her father. Like the father of the Brontës, the father of the Barretts is one of the enigmas of literary history;

he was a factor of overwhelming importance in that strange family. Chesterton says 'at last . . . she knew to all intents and purposes that she had grown up in the house of a madman.'

To his children he was almost unbelievably despotic; and, especially, any suggestion of the possibility of marriage for any one of them seems to have driven him to fury. 'Everyone you see . . . all my brothers . . . constrained *bodily* into submission . . . by that worst and most dishonouring of necessities, the necessity of *living*, everyone of them all, except myself, being dependent in money matters on the inflexible will.' But though she realised that her father was 'a peculiar person', it is clear that for many years Elizabeth was genuinely devoted to him. Two crises in her life, before their final parting, affected her feelings towards him. The first was the death of her brother Edward—'my brother whom I loved so . . . the dearest of friends and brothers in one . . . better than us all, and kindest and noblest and dearest to *me*, beyond comparison, any comparison . . .' After their mother died, the family had moved to Sidmouth, and then to London, where Elizabeth became very ill. 'They sent me down you know to Torquay—Dr Chambers saying that I could not live a winter in London. The worst—what people call the worst—was apprehended for me at that time. So I was sent down with my sister to my aunt there—and he, my brother whom I loved so, was sent too, to take us there and return.' But when the time came for his return Elizabeth was so distressed that her father with great reluctance allowed him to remain, though he 'considered it to be *very wrong in me to exact such a thing.*' Then, two years later, Edward was drowned at sea! it nearly killed Elizabeth. 'For three days we waited —and I hoped while I could—oh—that awful agony of three days! . . . I, who could not speak or shed a tear, but lay for weeks and months half conscious, half unconscious, with a wandering mind . . . The spring of life . . . seemed to break within me *then.*' Her sensitive imagination accused her with 'acrid thoughts.' 'For see how it was, and how, "not with my hand but heart," I was the cause or occasion of that misery—and though not with the intention of my heart but with its weakness, yet the *occasion*, any way!' This tragedy in her life brought her father very near to her: 'When . . . I lost what I loved best in the world beyond comparison and rivalship . . . far better than himself as he knew . . . when I lost *that*, . . . I felt that he stood the nearest to me on the closed grave . . . or by the unclosing sea . . . he was generous and forbearing in that hour of bitter trial, and never reproached me as he might have done and as my own soul has not spared.'

In the Dedication 'T o M y F a t h e r' prefixed to the first edition of her P o e m s she says: 'You, who have shared with me in things bitter and sweet, softening or enhancing them, every day . . . may accept from me the inscription of these volumes, the exponents of a few years of an existence which has been sustained and comforted by you as well as given . . . It is my fancy thus . . . to satisfy my heart while I sanctify my ambition, by associating with the great pursuit of my life its tenderest and holiest affection.'

This is not the language of one oppressed beyond endurance, and at this time her father can hardly have been, to Elizabeth at least, the monster he has been represented; and it is worth remembering, perhaps, that this pathetic Dedication was reprinted in all editions of her Poems till her death—long after she had left him, never to be forgiven.

In 1841 she returned to Wimpole Street, to lead there for many years her invalid life, shut in her room, with 'Flush, my dog' her chief companion and 'loving friend.'

> But of *thee* it shall be said,
> This dog watched beside a bed
>   Day and night unweary,
> Watched within a curtained room
> Where no sunbeam brake the gloom
>   Round the sick and dreary.

In the summer she would go out sometimes in a chair or carriage, or even, very rarely, for a walk. 'I was out walking again to-day, and . . . I walked up all these stairs with my own feet on returning. I sate down on the stairs two or three times . . . and I was not carried, as usual—see how vain-glorious I am.'

But in the winters she could hardly leave her room: 'We all get used to the thought of a tomb, and I was buried, that was the whole.' The second crisis in her relations with her father occurred after she and Browning had met, and must have made easier for her the decision to escape.

His character was 'becoming gloomier and stranger as time went on' * and though in July 1845 he was 'discussing the question' of sending Elizabeth abroad for the winter—'though . . . I suppose, *I* should not be much consulted'—yet in September, when her doctor urged the necessity of it, he deliberately made her going impossible. 'Words have been said that I cannot easily forget, nor remember without pain . . . I told him that my prospects of health seemed to me to depend on taking this step . . . I feel aggrieved of course and wounded.' Later she writes: 'I had believed Papa to have loved me more than he obviously does'; and again: 'If he had let me I should have loved him . . . Now it is too late . . .'

This weakening of her affection for her father must

* G. K. Chesterton, *Robert Browning*.

have influenced her later conduct profoundly, yet even before this time the greater influence of Browning had altered her whole outlook. They knew nothing of each other beyond their published works, but a common admiration served as introduction. 'I love your verses with all my heart, dear Miss Barrett'—so begins one of the most fascinating correspondences in English literature.

This was in January 1845, and by May after many letters and much hesitation on her part, Browning had overcome her 'blind dislike of seeing strangers' and was admitted to see her for the first time. Two days later she received a letter—the only one in the long series to be destroyed—which must have amounted to a declaration of love. Her answer is preserved: 'You do not know what pain you give me in speaking so wildly. You have said some intemperate things . . . fancies,—which you will *forget at once,* and *for ever,* having said at all . . . if there should be one word of answer attempted to this; or of reference; *I must not . . . I will not see you again.*' But, on this condition, he might call on Tuesday.

He did call, and they continued to meet secretly once a week, until in September she wrote: 'You have touched me more profoundly than I thought even *you* could have touched me . . . Henceforward I am yours for everything but to do you harm.' For a full year more their meetings went on; both writing almost daily, and sometimes twice a day; Browning urging her to marry him and fly to Italy, Elizabeth consenting but hesitant. 'I will do what you please and as you please to have it done. But there is time for considering.' During this time she must have been writing the Sonnets, but there is no mention of them in her letters. It was not lack of courage in either that made it impossible to face her father, but the absolute certainty of his refusal. 'He would rather see me dead at his foot . . . We should be separated, you see, from *that moment.*'

A secret elopement was the only possibility. *'Elopement*—(But, dearest, nobody will use such a word surely to the *event.*)' At last the time came when they must decide at once, or wait another year—Elizabeth's health would not allow a winter journey. They were married on Saturday, September 12th, 1846, and she returned to Wimpole Street after the service: a week later, with Flush and her maid Wilson, they sailed for France. She never saw her father again; when, years later, they came back to England, the letters she had written him were sent to her unopened: Wimpole Street was closed against her. From Paris they went to Pisa, and there for the first time she showed the Sonnets to her husband. There is, of course, no Portuguese original for them. Browning admired especially her poem 'Catarina to Camoens,' and had called her his 'little Portuguese.' It has been suggested that this may have been the origin of the purposely misleading title, which was not used until the Sonnets were published in 1850. Referring to their publication Browning is reported to have said: 'I dared not keep to myself the finest Sonnets written in any language since Shakespeare's.'

SONNETS
FROM
THE PORTUGUESE

I

I thought once how Theocritus had sung
Of the sweet years, the dear and wished for years,
Who each one in a gracious hand appears
To bear a gift for mortals, old or young:
And, as I mused it in his antique tongue,
I saw, in gradual vision through my tears,
The sweet, sad years, the melancholy years,
Those of my own life, who by turns had flung
A shadow across me. Straightway I was 'ware,
So weeping, how a mystic Shape did move
Behind me, and drew me backward by the hair,
And a voice said in mastery while I strove, . .
'Guess now who holds thee?'—'Death,' I said. But, there,
The silver answer rang . . 'Not Death, but Love.'

II

But only three in all God's universe
Have heard this word thou hast said,—Himself, beside
Thee speaking, and me listening! and replied
One of us .. *that* was God, .. and laid the curse
So darkly on my eyelids, as to amerce
My sight from seeing thee,—that if I had died,
The deathweights, placed there, would have signified
Less absolute exclusion. 'Nay' is worse
From God than from all others, O my friend!
Men could not part us with their worldly jars,
Nor the seas change us, nor the tempests bend;
Our hands would touch for all the mountain-bars,—
And, heaven being rolled between us at the end,
We should but vow the faster for the stars.

III

Unlike are we, unlike, O princely Heart!
Unlike our uses and our destinies.
Our ministering two angels look surprise
On one another, as they strike athwart
Their wings in passing. Thou, bethink thee, art
A guest for queens to social pageantries,
With gages from a hundred brighter eyes
Than tears even can make mine, to ply* thy part
Of chief musician. What hast *thou* to do
With looking from the lattice-lights at me,
A poor, tired, wandering singer, . . singing through
The dark, and leaning up a cypress tree?
The chrism is on thine head,—on mine, the dew,—
And Death must dig the level where these agree.

* Altered to *play* in later editions.

IV

Thou hast thy calling to some palace-floor,
Most gracious singer of high poems! where
The dancers will break footing, from the care
Of watching up thy pregnant lips for more.
And dost thou lift this house's latch too poor
For hand of thine? and canst thou think and bear
To let thy music drop here unaware
In folds of golden fulness at my door?
Look up and see the casement broken in,
The bats and owlets builders in the roof!
My cricket chirps against thy mandolin.
Hush, call no echo up in further proof
Of desolation! there's a voice within
That weeps . . as thou must sing . . alone, aloof.

V

I lift my heavy heart up solemnly,
As once Electra her sepulchral urn,
And, looking in thine eyes, I overturn
The ashes at thy feet. Behold and see
What a great heap of grief lay hid in me,
And how the red wild sparkles dimly burn
Through the ashen greyness. If thy foot in scorn
Could tread them out to darkness utterly,
It might be well perhaps. But if instead
Thou wait beside me for the wind to blow
The grey dust up, . . . those laurels on thine head,
O my belov'd, will not shield thee so,
That none of all the fires shall scorch and shred
The hair beneath. Stand further off then! go.

VI

Go from me. Yet I feel that I shall stand
Henceforward in thy shadow. Nevermore
Alone upon the threshold of my door
Of individual life, I shall command
The uses of my soul, nor lift my hand
Serenely in the sunshine as before,
Without the sense of that which I forbore, . .
Thy touch upon the palm. The widest land
Doom takes to part us, leaves thy heart in mine
With pulses that beat double. What I do
And what I dream include thee, as the wine
Must taste of its own grapes. And when I sue
God for myself, He hears that name of thine,
And sees within my eyes, the tears of two.

VII

The face of all the world is changed, I think,
Since first I heard the footsteps of thy soul
Move still, oh, still, beside me, as they stole
Betwixt me and the dreadful outer brink
Of obvious death, where I, who thought to sink,
Was caught up into love, and taught the whole
Of life in a new rhythm. The cup of dole
God gave for baptism, I am fain to drink,
And praise its sweetness, Sweet, with thee anear.
The names of country, heaven, are changed away
For where thou art or shalt be, there or here;
And this . . this lute and song . . loved yesterday,
(The singing angels know) are only dear,
Because thy name moves right in what they say.

VIII

What can I give thee back, O liberal
And princely giver, who hast brought the gold
And purple of thine heart, unstained, untold,
And laid them on the outside of the wall
For such as I to take or leave withal,
In unexpected largesse? am I cold,
Ungrateful, that for these most manifold
High gifts, I render nothing back at all?
Not so; not cold,—but very poor instead.
Ask God who knows. For frequent tears have run
The colours from my life, and left so dead
And pale a stuff, it were not fitly done
To give the same as pillow to thy head.
Go farther! let it serve to trample on.

IX

Can it be right to give what I can give?
To let thee sit beneath the fall of tears
As salt as mine, and hear the sighing years
Re-sighing on my lips renunciative
Through those infrequent smiles which fail to live
For all thy adjurations? O my fears,
That this can scarce be right! We are not peers,
So to be lovers; and I own, and grieve,
That givers of such gifts as mine are, must
Be counted with the ungenerous. Out, alas!
I will not soil thy purple with my dust,
Nor breathe my poison on thy Venice-glass,
Nor give thee any love . . . which were unjust.
Beloved, I only love thee! let it pass.

X

Yet, love, mere love, is beautiful indeed
And worthy of acceptation. Fire is bright,
Let temple burn, or flax. An equal light
Leaps in the flame from cedar-plank or weed.
And love is fire; and when I say at need
I love thee . . mark! . . *I love thee!* . . in thy sight
I stand transfigured, glorified aright,
With conscience of the new rays that proceed
Out of my face toward thine. There's nothing low
In love, when love the lowest: meanest creatures
Who love God, God accepts while loving so.
And what I *feel*, across the inferior features
Of what I *am*, doth flash itself, and show
How that great work of Love enhances Nature's.

XI

And therefore if to love can be desert,
I am not all unworthy. Cheeks as pale
As these you see, and trembling knees that fail
To bear the burden of a heavy heart,—
This weary minstrel-life that once was girt
To climb Aornus, and can scarce avail
To pipe now 'gainst the valley nightingale
A melancholy music,—why advert
To these things? O Beloved, it is plain
I am not of thy worth nor for thy place!
And yet, because I love thee, I obtain
From that same love this vindicating grace,
To live on still in love, and yet in vain, . .
To bless thee, yet renounce thee to thy face.

XII

Indeed this very love which is my boast,
And which, when rising up from breast to brow,
Doth crown me with a ruby large enow
To draw men's eyes and prove the inner cost, . .
This love even, all my worth, to the uttermost,
I should not love withal, unless that thou
Hadst set me an example, shown me how,
When first thine earnest eyes with mine were crossed,
And love called love. And thus, I cannot speak
Of love even, as a good thing of my own.
Thy soul hath snatched up mine all faint and weak,
And placed it by thee on a golden throne,—
And that I love (O soul, we must be meek!)
Is by thee only, whom I love alone.

XIII

And wilt thou have me fashion into speech
The love I bear thee, finding words enough,
And hold the torch out, while the winds are rough,
Between our faces, to cast light on each?—
I drop it at thy feet. I cannot teach
My hand to hold my spirit so far off
From myself . . me . . that I should bring thee proof
In words, of love hid in me out of reach.
Nay, let the silence of my womanhood
Commend my woman-love to thy belief,—
Seeing that I stand unwon, however wooed,
And rend the garment of my life, in brief,
By a most dauntless, voiceless fortitude,
Lest one touch of this heart convey its grief.

XIV

If thou must love me, let it be for nought
Except for love's sake only. Do not say
'I love her for her smile . . her look . . her way
Of speaking gently, . . for a trick of thought
That falls in well with mine, and certes brought
A sense of pleasant ease on such a day'—
For these things in themselves, Belovèd, may
Be changed, or change for thee,—and love, so wrought,
May be unwrought so. Neither love me for
Thine own dear pity's wiping my cheeks dry,—
A creature might forget to weep, who bore
Thy comfort long, and lose thy love thereby!
But love me for love's sake, that evermore
Thou may'st love on, through love's eternity.

XV

Accuse me not, beseech thee, that I wear
Too calm and sad a face in front of thine;
For we two look two ways, and cannot shine
With the same sunlight on our brow and hair.
On me thou lookest, with no doubting care,
As on a bee shut in a crystalline,—
Since sorrow hath shut me safe in love's divine,
And to spread wing and fly in the outer air
Were most impossible failure, if I strove
To fail so. But I look on thee . . on thee . .
Beholding, besides love, the end of love,
Hearing oblivion beyond memory!
As one who sits and gazes from above,
Over the rivers to the bitter sea.

XVI

And yet, because thou overcomest so,
Because thou art more noble and like a king,
Thou canst prevail against my fears and fling
Thy purple round me, till my heart shall grow
Too close against thine heart, henceforth to know
How it shook when alone. Why, conquering
May prove as lordly and complete a thing
In lifting upward, as in crushing low!
And as a vanquished soldier yields his sword
To one who lifts him from the bloody earth,—
Even so, Belovèd, I at last record,
Here ends my strife. If *thou* invite me forth,
I rise above abasement at the word.
Make thy love larger to enlarge my worth.

XVII

My poet, thou canst touch on all the notes
God set between His After and Before,
And strike up and strike off the general roar
Of the rushing worlds, a melody that floats
In a serene air purely. Antidotes
Of medicated music, answering for
Mankind's forlornest uses, thou canst pour
From thence into their ears. God's will devotes
Thine to such ends, and mine to wait on thine.
How, Dearest, wilt thou have me for most use?
A hope, to sing by gladly? . . or a fine
Sad memory, with thy songs to interfuse?
A shade, in which to sing . . . of palm or pine?
A grave, on which to rest from singing? . . Choose.

XVIII

I never gave a lock of hair away
To a man, Dearest, except this to thee,
Which now upon my fingers thoughtfully
I ring out to the full brown length and say
'Take it.' My day of youth went yesterday;
My hair no longer bounds to my foot's glee,
Nor plant I it from rose or myrtle-tree,
As girls do, any more. It only may
Now shade on two pale cheeks, the mark of tears,
Taught drooping from the head that hangs aside
Through sorrow's trick. I thought the funeral-shears
Would take this first, but Love is justified,—
Take it thou, . . finding pure, from all those years,
The kiss my mother left here when she died.

XIX

The soul's Rialto hath its merchandise;
I barter curl for curl upon that mart,
And from my poet's forehead to my heart,
Receive this lock which outweighs argosies,—
As purply black, as erst, to Pindar's eyes,
The dim purpureal tresses gloomed athwart
The nine white Muse-brows. For this counterpart, . .
Thy bay-crown's shade, Belovèd, I surmise,
Still lingers on thy curl, it is so black!
Thus, with a fillet of smooth-kissing breath,
I tie the shadow safe from gliding back,
And lay the gift where nothing hindereth,
Here on my heart, as on thy brow, to lack
No natural heat till mine grows cold in death.

XX

Beloved, my Beloved, when I think
That thou wast in the world a year ago,
What time I sat alone here in the snow
And saw no footprint, heard the silence sink
No moment at thy voice, . . but, link by link,
Went counting all my chains, as if that so
They never could fall off at any blow
Struck by thy possible hand . . . . why, thus I drink
Of life's great cup of wonder! Wonderful,
Never to feel thee thrill the day or night
With personal act or speech,—nor ever cull
Some prescience of thee with the blossoms white
Thou sawest growing! Atheists are as dull,
Who cannot guess God's presence out of sight.

XXI

Say over again, and yet once over again,
That thou dost love me. Though the word repeated
Should seem 'a cuckoo-song,' as thou dost treat it.
Remember never to the hill or plain,
Valley and wood, without her cuckoo-strain,
Comes the fresh Spring in all her green completed.
Beloved, I, amid the darkness greeted
By a doubtful spirit-voice, in that doubt's pain
Cry . . 'Speak once more . . thou lovest!' Who can fear
Too many stars, though each in heaven shall roll—
Too many flowers, though each shall crown the year?
Say thou dost love me, love me, love me—toll
The silver iterance!—only minding, Dear,
To love me also in silence, with thy soul.

XXII

When our two souls stand up erect and strong,
Face to face, silent, drawing nigh and nigher,
Until the lengthening wings break into fire
At either curvèd point,—what bitter wrong
Can the earth do to us, that we should not long
Be here contented? Think. In mounting higher,
The angels would press on us, and aspire
To drop some golden orb of perfect song
Into our deep, dear silence. Let us stay
Rather on earth, Belovèd,—where the unfit
Contrarious moods of men recoil away
And isolate pure spirits, and permit
A place to stand and love in for a day,
With darkness and the death-hour rounding it.

XXIII

Is it indeed so? If I lay here dead,
Would'st thou miss any life in losing mine?
And would the sun for thee more coldly shine,
Because of grave-damps falling round my head?
I marvelled, my Belovèd, when I read
Thy thought so in the letter. I am thine—
But . . *so* much to thee? Can I pour thy wine
While my hands tremble? Then my soul, instead
Of dreams of death, resumes life's lower range.
Then, love me, Love! look on me . . breathe on me!
As brighter ladies do not count it strange,
For love, to give up acres and degree,
I yield the grave for thy sake, and exchange
My near sweet view of Heaven, for earth with thee!

XXIV

Let the world's sharpness like a clasping knife
Shut in upon itself and do no harm
In this close hand of Love, now soft and warm,
And let us hear no sound of human strife
After the click of the shutting. Life to life—
I lean upon thee, Dear, without alarm,
And feel as safe as guarded by a charm
Against the stab of worldlings, who if rife
Are weak to injure. Very whitely still
The lilies of our lives may reassure
Their blossoms from their roots, accessible
Alone to heavenly dews that drop not fewer;
Growing straight, out of man's reach, on the hill.
God only, who made us rich, can make us poor.

XXV

A heavy heart, Belovèd, have I borne
From year to year until I saw thy face,
And sorrow after sorrow took the place
Of all those natural joys as lightly worn
As the stringed pearls . . each lifted in its turn
By a beating heart at dance-time. Hopes apace
Were changed to long despairs, till God's own grace
Could scarcely lift above the world forlorn
My heavy heart. Then *thou* didst bid me bring
And let it drop adown thy calmly great
Deep being! Fast it sinketh, as a thing
Which its own nature doth precipitate,
While thine doth close above it, mediating
Betwixt the stars and the unaccomplished fate.

XXVI

I lived with visions for my company,
Instead of men and women, years ago,
And found them gentle mates, nor thought to know
A sweeter music than they played to me.
But soon their trailing purple was not free
Of this world's dust,—their lutes did silent grow,
And I myself grew faint and blind below
Their vanishing eyes. Then THOU didst come . . to be,
Belovèd, what they seemed. Their shining fronts,
Their songs, their splendours, (better, yet the same,
As river-water hallowed into fonts)
Met in thee, and from out thee overcame
My soul with satisfaction of all wants—
Because God's gifts put man's best dreams to shame.

XXVII

My own belovèd, who hast lifted me
From this drear flat of earth where I was thrown,
And, in betwixt the languid ringlets, blown
A life-breath, till the forehead hopefully
Shines out again, as all the angels see,
Before thy saving kiss! My own, my own,
Who camest to me when the world was gone,
And I who looked for only God, found *thee!*
I find thee; I am safe, and strong, and glad.
As one who stands in dewless asphodel,
Looks backward on the tedious time he had
In the upper life,—so I, with bosom-swell,
Make witness, here, between the good and bad,
That Love, as strong as Death, retrieves as well.

XXVIII

My letters! all dead paper, . . mute and white—
And yet they seem alive and quivering
Against my tremulous hands which loose the string
And let them drop down on my knee to-night.
This said, . . he wished to have me in his sight
Once, as a friend: this fixed a day in spring
To come and touch my hand . . . a simple thing,
Yet I wept for it!—this, . . the paper's light . .
Said, *Dear, I love thee;* and I sank and quailed
As if God's future thundered on my past.
This said, *I am thine*—and so its ink has paled
With lying at my heart that beat too fast.
And this . . . O Love, thy words have ill availed,
If, what this said, I dared repeat at last!

XXIX

I think of thee!—my thoughts do twine and bud
About thee, as wild vines, about a tree,
Put out broad leaves, and soon there's nought to see
Except the straggling green which hides the wood.
Yet, O my palm-tree, be it understood
I will not have my thoughts instead of thee
Who art dearer, better! rather instantly
Renew thy presence. As a strong tree should,
Rustle thy boughs and set thy trunk all bare,
And let these bands of greenery which insphere thee,
Drop heavily down, . . burst, shattered, everywhere!
Because, in this deep joy to see and hear thee
And breathe within thy shadow a new air,
I do not think of thee—I am too near thee.

XXX

I see thine image through my tears to-night,
And yet to-day I saw thee smiling. How
Refer the cause?—Belovèd, is it thou
Or I? who makes me sad? The acolyte
Amid the chanted joy and thankful rite,
May so fall flat, with pale insensate brow,
On the altar-stair. I hear thy voice and vow
Perplexed, uncertain, since thou art out of sight,
As he, in his swooning ears, the choir's amen.
Belovèd, dost thou love? or did I see all
The glory as I dreamed, and fainted when
Too vehement light dilated my ideal,
For my soul's eyes? Will that light come again,
As now these tears come . . . falling hot and real?

XXXI

Thou comest! all is said without a word.
I sit beneath thy looks, as children do
In the noon-sun, with souls that tremble through
Their happy eyelids from an unaverred
Yet prodigal inward joy. Behold, I erred
In that last doubt! and yet I cannot rue
The sin most, but the occasion . . . that we two
Should for a moment stand unministered
By a mutual presence. Ah, keep near and close,
Thou dovelike help! and, when my fears would rise,
With thy broad heart serenely interpose.
Brood down with thy divine sufficiencies
These thoughts which tremble when bereft of those,
Like callow birds left desert to the skies.

XXXII

The first time that the sun rose on thine oath
To love me, I looked forward to the moon
To slacken all those bonds which seemed too soon
And quickly tied to make a lasting troth.
Quick-loving hearts, I thought, may quickly loathe;
And, looking on myself, I seemed not one
For such man's love!—more like an out-of-tune
Worn viol, a good singer would be wroth
To spoil his song with, and which, snatched in haste,
Is laid down at the first ill-sounding note.
I did not wrong myself so, but I placed
A wrong on *thee*. For perfect strains may float
'Neath master-hands, from instrument defaced,—
And great souls, at one stroke, may do and doat.

XXXIII

Yes, call me by my pet-name! let me hear
The name I used to run at, when a child,
From innocent play, and leave the cowslips piled,
To glance up in some face that proved me dear
With the look of its eyes. I miss the clear
Fond voices which, being drawn and reconciled
Into the music of Heaven's undefiled,
Call me no longer. Silence on the bier,
While I call God . . call God!—So let thy mouth
Be heir to those who are now exanimate.
Gather the north flowers to complete the south,
And catch the early love up in the late.
Yes, call me by that name,—and I, in truth,
With the same heart, will answer, and not wait.

XXXIV

With the same heart, I said, I'll answer thee
As those, when thou shalt call me by my name—
Lo, the vain promise! is the same, the same,
Perplexed and ruffled by life's strategy?
When called before, I told how hastily
I dropped my flowers or brake off from a game,
To run and answer with the smile that came
At play last moment, and went on with me
Through my obedience. When I answer now,
I drop a grave thought,—break from solitude;—
Yet still my heart goes to thee . . . ponder how . .
Not as to a single good, but all my good!
Lay thy hand on it, best one, and allow
That no child's foot could run fast as this blood.

XXXV

If I leave all for thee, wilt thou exchange
And be all to me? Shall I never miss
Home-talk and blessing and the common kiss
That comes to each in turn, nor count it strange,
When I look up, to drop on a new range
Of walls and floors . . another home than this?
Nay, wilt thou fill that place by me which is
Filled by dead eyes too tender to know change?
That's hardest. If to conquer love, has tried,
To conquer grief, tries more . . . as all things prove;
For grief indeed is love and grief beside.
Alas, I have grieved so I am hard to love.
Yet love me—wilt thou? Open thine heart wide,
And fold within, the wet wings of thy dove.

XXXVI

When we met first and loved, I did not build
Upon the event with marble. Could it mean
To last, a love set pendulous between
Sorrow and sorrow? Nay, I rather thrilled,
Distrusting every light that seemed to gild
The onward path, and feared to overlean
A finger even. And, though I have grown serene
And strong since then, I think that God has willed
A still renewable fear . . O love, O troth . .
Lest these enclaspèd hands should never hold,
This mutual kiss drop down between us both
As an unowned thing, once the lips being cold.
And Love, be false! if *he*, to keep one oath,
Must lose one joy, by his life's star foretold.

XXXVII

Pardon, oh, pardon, that my soul should make
Of all that strong divineness which I know
For thine and thee, an image only so
Formed of the sand, and fit to shift and break.
It is that distant years which did not take
Thy sovranty, recoiling with a blow,
Have forced my swimming brain to undergo
Their doubt and dread, and blindly to forsake
Thy purity of likeness, and distort
Thy worthiest love to a worthless counterfeit.
As if a shipwrecked Pagan, safe in port,
His guardian sea-god to commemorate,
Should set a sculptured porpoise, gills a-snort,
And vibrant tail, within the temple-gate.

XXXVIII

First time he kissed me, he but only kissed
The fingers of this hand wherewith I write;
And, ever since, it grew more clean and white, . .
Slow to world-greetings . . quick with its 'Oh, list,'
When the angels speak. A ring of amethyst
I could not wear here, plainer to my sight,
Than that first kiss. The second passed in height
The first, and sought the forehead, and half missed,
Half falling on the hair. O beyond meed!
That was the chrism of love, which love's own crown,
With sanctifying sweetness, did precede.
The third upon my lips was folded down
In perfect, purple state; since when, indeed,
I have been proud and said, 'My love, my own.'

XXXIX

Because thou hast the power and own'st the grace
To look through and behind this mask of me,
(Against which years have beat thus blanchingly
With their rains), and behold my soul's true face,
The dim and weary witness of life's race!—
Because thou hast the faith and love to see,
Through that same soul's distracting lethargy,
The patient angel waiting for a place
In the new heavens!—because nor sin nor woe,
Nor God's infliction, nor death's neighbourhood,
Nor all which others viewing, turn to go, . .
Nor all which makes me tired of all, self-viewed, . .
Nothing repels thee, . . Dearest, teach me so
To pour out gratitude, as thou dost, good.

XL

Oh, yes! they love through all this world of ours!
I will not gainsay love, called love forsooth.
I have heard love talked in my early youth,
And since, not so long back but that the flowers
Then gathered, smell still. Mussulmans and Giaours
Throw kerchiefs at a smile, and have no ruth
For any weeping. Polypheme's white tooth
Slips on the nut, if, after frequent showers,
The shell is over-smooth,—and not so much
Will turn the thing called love, aside to hate,
Or else to oblivion. But thou art not such
A lover, my Belovèd! thou canst wait
Through sorrow and sickness, to bring souls to touch,
And think it soon when others cry 'Too late.'

XLI

I thank all who have loved me in their hearts,
With thanks and love from mine. Deep thanks to all
Who paused a little near the prison-wall,
To hear my music in its louder parts,
Ere they went onward, each one to the mart's
Or temple's occupation, beyond call.
But thou, who, in my voice's sink and fall,
When the sob took it, thy divinest Art's
Own instrument didst drop down at thy foot,
To hearken what I said between my tears, . .
Instruct me how to thank thee!—Oh, to shoot
My soul's full meaning into future years,
That *they* should lend it utterance, and salute
Love that endures, from Life that disappears!

XLII*

'*My future will not copy fair my past*'—
I wrote that once; and thinking at my side
My ministering life-angel justified
The word by his appealing look upcast
To the white throne of God, I turned at last,
And there, instead, saw thee, not unallied
To angels in thy soul! Then I, long tried
By natural ills, received the comfort fast,
While budding, at thy sight, my pilgrim's staff
Gave out green leaves with morning dews impearled.
I seek no copy now of life's first half:
Leave here the pages with long musing curled,
And write me new my future's epigraph,
New angel mine, unhoped for in the world!

   * This sonnet, originally called FUTURE AND PAST, was not included in the series in the earlier editions. See Note on the text, page 107.

XLIII

How do I love thee? Let me count the ways.
I love thee to the depth and breadth and height
My soul can reach, when feeling out of sight
For the ends of Being and ideal Grace.
I love thee to the level of everyday's
Most quiet need, by sun and candlelight.
I love thee freely, as men strive for Right;
I love thee purely, as they turn from Praise.
I love thee with the passion put to use
In my old griefs, and with my childhood's faith.
I love thee with a love I seemed to lose
With my lost saints,—I love thee with the breath,
Smiles, tears, of all my life!—and, if God choose,
I shall but love thee better after death.

XLIV

Belovèd, thou hast brought me many flowers
Plucked in the garden, all the summer through
And winter, and it seemed as if they grew
In this close room, nor missed the sun and showers.
So, in the like name of that love of ours,
Take back these thoughts which here unfolded too,
And which on warm and cold days I withdrew
From my heart's ground. Indeed, those beds and
    bowers
Be overgrown with bitter weeds and rue,
And wait thy weeding; yet here's eglantine,
Here's ivy!—take them, as I used to do
Thy flowers, and keep them where they shall not pine.
Instruct thine eyes to keep their colours true,
And tell thy soul, their roots are left in mine.

A NOTE ON THE TEXT

The present text is reprinted from that of the fourth edition of POEMS BY ELIZABETH BARRETT BROWNING published in 1856. This was the last edition published in the author's lifetime, and it contains her final revisions; the sonnet now numbered XLII was included in the series for the first time. The history of the previous editions is as follows. The first was privately printed, with the title-page SONNETS./ BY/ E. A. B./ READING: / [NOT FOR PUBLICATION] [rule] 1847. There is no copy of this very rare volume in the British Museum or in the Bodleian Library, but a facsimile of the title-page is given in T. J. Wise's Bibliography of the Writings . . . of Elizabeth Barrett Browning. In this and in all subsequent editions until that of 1856 the series consists of 43 sonnets only. The first edition of POEMS / BY / ELIZABETH BARRETT / was published by Edward Moxon in 1844. It contains one sonnet, PAST AND FUTURE, which is referred to in the

SONNETS FROM THE PORTUGUESE and is not being reprinted in the present edition. The second edition of POEMS / BY / ELIZABETH BARRETT BROWNING / was published in 1850 by Chapman and Hall. It contains the first public issue of the 43 sonnets, here first called SONNETS FROM THE PORTUGUESE, and also the present number XLII which was printed apart from the series, with the title FUTURE AND PAST. The third edition of POEMS was published in 1853 and has the following 'Postscript', dated from Florence: 'In the present edition the author has done her best to remedy the oversights and defects of that former revision [1850] which her absence from England rendered less complete than it should have been. This revision did not greatly affect the SONNETS FROM THE PORTUGUESE. A few alterations were made, but the more important variations were not included until the next edition. In the fourth edition of the POEMS, published in 1856, the SONNETS FROM THE PORTUGUESE appeared for the first time in their present form. FUTURE AND PAST was added to the series as No. XLII, without other title, bringing the total number of the sonnets to 44; and various alterations were made from the text of the first public issue of 1850, the more interesting of which are recorded below.

SONNET XI. l. 7

To pipe now 'gainst the valley nightingale	1856
. . . the woodland nightingale	1850

SONNET XII. l. 13

And that I love (O soul, we must be meek!)	1856
. . . I must be meek!)	1850

SONNET XIV. l. 11

A creature might forget to weep, who bore	1856
Since one might well forget to weep, who bore	1850

SONNET XV. l. 7

Since sorrow hath shut me safe in love's divine	1856
For sorrow . . .	1850

SONNET XVI. ll. 9-12

And as a vanquished soldier yields his sword To one who lifts him from the bloody earth,— Even so, Belovèd, I at last record, Here ends my strife.	1856

And, as a soldier struck down by a sword
May cry, 'My strife ends here,' and sink to earth,
Even so, Belovèd, I at last record,
Here ends my doubt.   1850

SONNET XXXVII. l. 10

. . . distort
Thy worthiest love to a worthless counterfeit.   1856
. . . with worthless counterfeit: 1850

SONNET XXXIX. l. 3

(Against which years have beat thus blanchingly 1856
. . . blenchingly 1850

SONNET XXXIX. l. 8

The patient angel waiting for a place   1856
. . . his place   1850

SONNET XLI. l. 14

. . . salute
Love that endures, from Life that disappears!   1856
. . . with Life that disappears!   1850

SONNET XLII. l. 6

And there, instead, saw thee, not unallied   1856
And saw instead there, *thee;* not unallied   1850